Celine Dion

Julia Holt

Published in association with The Basic Skills Agency

Hodder & Stoughton

A MEMBER OF THE HODDER HEADLINE GROUP

Acknowledgements

Cover: © P P Poulin/Corbis Sygma

Photos: p 2 Imapress/Camera Press; p 6 Theodore Wood/Camera Press; p 4, Frank Spooner; p 12 Mauro Carraro/Gamma/Frank Spooner; p 16 Topham Picturepoint; © Disney Enterprises, Inc.; p 21 Nahas/Ponopresse/Frank Spooner; p 27 Graham Whitby Boot/Allstar

Illustration p 14 Maureen Carter

Every effort has been made to trace copyright holders of material reproduced in this book. Any rights not acknowledged will be acknowledged in subsequent printings if notice is given to the publisher.

Orders: please contact Bookpoint Ltd, 39 Milton Park, Abingdon, Oxon OX14 4TD. Telephone: (44) 01235 400414, Fax: (44) 01235 400454. Lines are open from 9.00–6.00, Monday to Saturday, with a 24 hour message answering service. Email address: orders@bookpoint.co.uk

British Library Cataloguing in Publication Data
A catalogue record for this title is available from the British Library

ISBN 0 340 77621 8

First published 2000
Impression number   10 9 8 7 6 5 4 3 2 1
Year   2005 2004 2003 2002 2001 2000

Copyright © 2000 Julia Holt

Typeset by GreenGate Publishing Services, Tonbridge, Kent.
Printed in Great Britain for Hodder and Stoughton Educational, a division of Hodder Headline Plc, 338 Euston Road, London NW1 3BH, by Redwood Books, Trowbridge, Wilts

Contents

Celine Dion is going to have the year 2000 off work.

Her plan is to rest for a while. Her dream is to have a baby. So, after her New Year's Eve Millennium show in Canada, her year off will start.

Celine Dion.

1 Childhood

Celine's voice is world famous.
She has come a long, long way
from a small town
in Canada.

She was born into a rural family
on 30 March 1968.
Her first name is the title of a song.
Her mother sang it when she was pregnant.
Celine is the youngest
of 14 children.

Celine with her parents.

The family had to struggle
to make ends meet.
They only had the money
their father made as a butcher.

They lived in a four-bedroomed house.
There was one bedroom for five boys
and two bedrooms for nine girls.
All their clothes were washed by their mother
in the bath.

Celine learned to sing with the others
in the cellar of their house.
When she was five
she sang at her brother Michel's wedding.
Her father says,
'Her voice made people dance'.

Celine's parents opened a piano bar
called 'The Old Barrel'.
Father played the violin.
All the children waited on tables and sang.
When Celine was ten
they let her sing too.
Later she learned
to play the piano.

She used to say,
'I'm going to go out on tour
and be the biggest singer
in the world.'

2 Celine Meets Rene

Two years later Celine recorded a song
called *It Was Only A Dream*.
It was written by her mother.
They sent a tape of the song
to a well known manager
called Rene Angelil.
It was the song that changed her life.

Rene Angelil – her manager and future husband.

Rene liked Celine's voice.
He met the skinny twelve year old.
Rene told her mother,
'Within five years
she's going to be
the biggest artist in Quebec.'
It only took two.

Rene put all his money
into making two albums with Celine.
The French-speaking world
loved her songs.
In 1983 she became the first Canadian
to have a gold record in France.

As soon as she finished school
Celine toured Quebec.
She said she wanted
to be as big as Michael Jackson.
Rene made her take eighteen months off.
She learned English
and had a total make over.
Her mother says, 'In those months
she turned into a young woman.'

3 Her Singing Career Begins

By the time Celine was twenty
she was a superstar in Canada.
In Dublin that year
she won the Eurovision Song Contest
for Switzerland.
The world was getting to know her.

As her career grew, so did her love for Rene.
He is twenty-six years older than her.
He had divorced his second wife in 1985.
His three children
are all older than Celine.
They chose not to tell the public
about their love.

Singing for Switzerland.

Celine's rise to world superstar began in 1990
with her first album in English.
It was called *Unison*.
It sold two million copies.

That year Celine and Rene opened the first
of a chain of forty-four restaurants.
The chain is called *Nickels*.
One thing on the menu
is a six layer chocolate cake called *Celine*.

Celine's lucky number is five
because she found a five cent coin one day.
A five cent coin in Canada
is made from nickel.
So that's what they called their restaurants.

Nickels restaurant.

4 Her Big Break

Celine's big break came in 1991.
It was the first
of her many famous film tracks.
It was the title track
from Disney's *Beauty and the Beast*.

The song went to No 1
and won an Oscar.
Celine put it on her second album
in English.
The album was called simply *Celine Dion*.
She had four more hits
from that album.

Beauty and the Beast. © Disney Enterprises, Inc.

Sony and Celine made a contract
to make five albums over ten years.
The contract was worth $10 million.
Celine made those five albums
in only five years.
Her feet hardly touched the ground.
She worked very hard.

When she goes on tour
she takes 105 people with her.
They all travel on their own jet.
Her brother Michel is her tour director.
Her sister Manon is her hairdresser.
She also takes some of her 500 pairs of shoes.

5 Love for Rene

In 1992 Rene had a heart attack.
Celine was with him.
She had just been swimming.
She went with Rene to the hospital
still in her swim suit.
Happily he soon got better.

They felt that they needed
to tell the public about their love.
They chose to do it
on the sleeve of her next album.
Celine wrote on the sleeve,
'Rene, you're the colour of my love'.
The album came out in 1993
and it was called *The Colour Of My Love*.

Celine and Rene
were worried she might lose fans
when they read the sleeve.
But she didn't.
She became one of the top female artists
of all time.
The album went to No 1 in Britain
and it stayed there for five weeks.
It sold 12 million copies.

Again she had a film track
on the album.
This time it was 'When I Fall In Love'
from the film *Sleepless in Seattle*.
A single from the album
called 'Think Twice'
stayed at No 1 for seven weeks.
She now had a million-selling single.

6 The Wedding

Canada had its own
'royal wedding' in December 1994.
It was the wedding
of Celine and Rene.
There were 500 guests
and all the family
had a police escort.

Their love is so strong that
in 1999, they read their wedding vows
again at a special ceremony.
Celine and Rene
live in a four-bedroomed house
in Canada.
They live there with her parents.
They also have
a $10 million house in Florida.

Celine and Rene were married in December 1994.

7 'Falling Into You'

Celine's album *Falling Into You*
came out in March 1996.
There were no adverts.
It was just put on the shelves.
It became a best-seller within weeks.
It went to the top of the charts in eleven countries
and it sold 25 million copies.

One song on this album is called 'Fly'.
Celine sang this song
for her niece Karine.
She died, aged sixteen,
of cystic fibrosis.
Celine now works hard
for cystic fibrosis groups
in memory of Karine.

As soon as the album came out,
Celine set off
on her *Falling Into You* world tour.

In July she took time out
to sing at the opening
of the Olympics in Atlanta.
She sang 'The Power Of The Dream'
in front of 3½ billion TV viewers.
She gave away her wage for the day
to the Canadian team.

Then she went on with her tour.
In total she gave 116 shows in 1996.

8 Time for the Family

Celine ended 1996
by giving her family
$100,000 each for Christmas.
She also let all of her
twenty-eight nieces and nephews
choose any toys they wanted.
Celine says,
'Christmas is my favourite time of year.'

1997 saw the end
of her sixteen month long tour.
In March she sang
two songs at the Oscars.
She was also on the famous *Oprah* TV show
with all her family.

9 World Wide Success

After her long tour
Celine rested by learning to play golf.

Sony gave Celine a contract
to make more albums
for a reported $75 million.
So she couldn't rest for long.

She records her songs in five languages.
Including Japanese.
She is very popular in Japan.

In November 1997
her fifth English album came out.
It was called *Let's Talk About Love*.
Again it was a big success.
She is joined on the album
by many other famous singers
like The Bee Gees.
In December
she sang in London for the Queen.

Then the film *Titanic*
came out in the US.

Celine sang the title track
for *Titanic*.
It was called
'My Heart Will Go On'.
Celine was at the top of her career.

In January 1999 Celine won the People's Choice Award for best singer.

She won many more awards
with the song from *Titanic*.

Since Celine's album of 1990, *Unison*,
she has made a total of 11 albums.
She has sold a total of 100 million albums.
In the past year
she has sold an album every 12 seconds.
Some say that she is worth $200 million.

It is no surprise
that she wants to take a year off.
As she says,
'I can't wait to do the normal things.
I'm looking forward to getting bored.'

As soon as she finishes
her *Let's Talk About Love* tour
she can do just that.